WHAT AM I?

Bright, Lively, and Loud

WHAT AM I?

By Moira Butterfield
Illustrated by Wayne Ford

RSVP
RAINTREE
STECK-VAUGHN
P U B L I S H E R S
The Steck-Vaughn Company

Austin, Texas

Published by Raintree Steck-Vaughn Publishers, an imprint of Steck-Vaughn Company.

Editors: Stephanie Bellwood, Heather Luff
Project Manager: Joyce Spicer
Designer: Helen James
Illustrator: Wayne Ford / Wildlife Art Agency
Consultant: Andrew Branson

Library of Congress Cataloging-in-Publication Data

Butterfield, Moira, 1961-
    Bright, Lively, and Loud/by Moira Butterfield; illustrated by Wayne Ford.
        p.   cm. — (What am I?)
    Summary: Gives basic information about the life of a parrot, written in the form of a riddle.
    ISBN 0-8172-4590-1 (hardcover)
    ISBN 0-8172-7227-5 (softcover)
    1. Parrots — Juvenile literature.   [1. Parrots.]
I. Ford, Wayne.   II. Title.   III. Series.
QL696.P7B88   1998
598.7'1 — dc21   96-54599
                                                       CIP   AC

Printed in Hong Kong
Bound in the United States.
1 2 3 4 5 6 7 8 9 0 WO 01 00 99 98 97

I am red and yellow,
green and blue.
I have wings and feathers, too.
My hooked beak
can crack a shell.
I eat fruit and nuts as well.

What am I?

Here is my beak.

I use it to crack open hard nutshells. Then I lick out the soft, tasty nut with my strong tongue.

When I see my friends, I make small clicking noises with my beak to say hello.

7

Here is my foot.

I am good at climbing trees and picking up things with my feet. Can you see some fruit for me to grab?

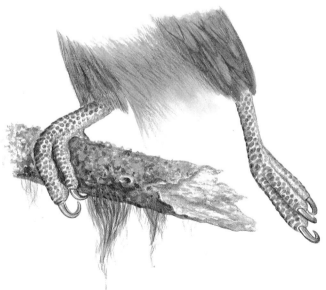

My curly toes can grip this branch tightly. Every now and then I stretch one of my scaly legs.

9

Here is my eye.

I must have a sharp eye to watch out for my enemies. That hungry snake wants to eat my eggs.

If this giant harpy eagle sees me, it will swoop down and catch me for dinner. I better stay hidden.

Here is my tail.

I keep my long tail
feathers very clean.
I spread them out
and comb each
one with my beak.

Here I am in a tree
with some of my
friends. How many
tails can you see
hanging down?

Here is my wing.

My wings are long and strong. When I open them wide and flap them, I can soar up into the air.

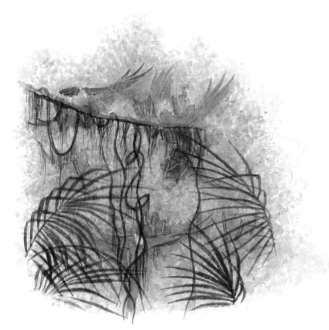

As I fly along, I look for fruits and nuts to eat. Perhaps there is some food in this tree.

15

Here are my feathers.

They look bright
and beautiful as I fly
through the jungle.
What other animals
can you see?

Sometimes it rains
very hard where I
live. When the rain
stops, my feathers
dry out in the sun.

17

Here is my home.

It is inside a hole in a tree trunk.
My home is easy to find because
I like to make lots of noise.

I open my beak and...
screech!
Have you guessed what I am?

I am a parrot.

Point to my...

hooked beak.

small eye.

curly toes.

colored feathers.

long tail.

strong wings.

I am called a
scarlet macaw.

Here are my babies.

They are called
chicks, and they
hatch from eggs.
I bring food to the
tree hole for them.

When they are
older, they grow
feathers. Then
they can fly high
above the trees,
just like me.

This is where I live.

It is a hot, rainy jungle
called the rain forest.

Can you find a toucan, four butterflies, a sloth, and a snake called an emerald tree boa?

Here is a map of the world.

I live in a place called South America where it is very hot. Can you find it on the map?

South America

Can you point to the
place where you live?

Can you answer these questions about me?

What do I like to eat?

How many colors are there on my feathers?

What do I use my strong beak for?

What is the weather like where I live?

What do I use
my feet for?

Where do I make
my home?

Who else lives in
the jungle with me?

What are my
babies called?

29

Here are words to help you learn about me.

beak My hard, hooked mouth. It is good for cracking nuts.

feathers Feathers are made up of many tiny, soft strands. My feathers are a lot of different colors.

grip To hold on very tightly.

hatch To break out of an egg. Baby birds are born this way.

hooked Curved, like my beak.

nutshell The hard coating of a nut. I use my beak to crack it.

rain forest My jungle home, where it is always hot and rainy.

scaly Dry and rough, like the skin on my legs.

soar The way I stretch my wings and fly up high.